Every
by Susan Lun...g

"This book sheds light on the often unspoken sensitivities and issues that women wrestle with. Not only is it well written, it is liberating and refreshing with sound principles for overcoming the things that threaten to keep us from experiencing the fullness of joy that is part of God's big-picture plan for our lives."

 —MICHELLE MCKINNEY HAMMOND, author of *Get Over It*
  and On With It

"In today's permissive culture, it is dangerously easy for even the most principled of women to reason away unhealthy thoughts, attitudes, and flirtations with men who aren't our husbands. In *Every Woman's Battle,* Shannon Ethridge bravely and respectfully draws a line in the sand for all of us. A must-read for every woman who desires true intimacy and sexual integrity."

 —CONSTANCE RHODES, author of *Life Inside the "Thin" Cage*

"There is a common, almost Victorian, myth that women don't really struggle with sexual sin. That myth causes many women to feel a double-shame. The shame of struggling sexually is compounded by the assumption that few, if any, women share the same battle. Shannon Ethridge artfully and boldly unveils the war and offers women a way to enter the battle with courage, hope, and grace. *Every Woman's Battle* will help both men and women comprehend the glorious beauty and sensuality of holiness. This is a desperately needed book."

 —Dr. DAN B. ALLENDER, president of Mars Hill Graduate School
  and author of *The Healing Path*

"If you're like me, you want the deepest connection possible with your husband. You want a soul-to-soul connection that is not encumbered by anything that could damage it. And if you're like me, you are going to find Shannon's book immeasurably helpful in doing just that. *Every Woman's Battle* is the best resource I know for embracing God's plan of sexual and emotional integrity as a woman."

—LESLIE PARROTT, author of *When Bad Things Happen to Good Marriages*

"A powerful shield for every woman. Shannon's words are convicting, challenging, and confronting."

—DR. TIM CLINTON, president of the American Association of Christian Counselors

"Many of my *Bad Girls of the Bible* readers have tearfully confessed to me their struggles with sexual sins—promiscuity, adultery, and self-gratification among them. Since we cannot pretend Christian women don't face these temptations, it's a relief to have a sound resource like this one to recommend. Shannon Ethridge's straightforward, nonjudgmental, step-by-step approach can help women come clean in the best way possible—through an intimate relationship with the Lover of their souls."

—LIZ CURTIS HIGGS, best-selling author of *Bad Girls of the Bible, Really Bad Girls of the Bible,* and *Mad Mary: A Bad Girl from Magdala*

"It's time to take the blinders off and recognize the crucial message of *Every Woman's Battle.*"

—KAREN KINGSBURY, best-selling author of *Remember* and *One Tuesday Morning*

Shannon Ethridge
with Foreword by **Stephen Arterburn**

every woman's battle

Discovering God's Plan for Sexual and Emotional Fulfillment

workbook

A Guide for Personal or Group Study

WATERBROOK
PRESS

EVERY WOMAN'S BATTLE WORKBOOK
PUBLISHED BY WATERBROOK PRESS
2375 Telstar Drive, Suite 160
Colorado Springs, Colorado 80920
A division of Random House, Inc.

Quotations from *Every Woman's Battle* © 2003 by Shannon Ethridge.

All Scripture quotations, unless otherwise indicated, are taken from *The Holy Bible, New International Version®*. NIV®. Copyright © 1973, 1978, 1984 by International Bible Society. Used by permission of Zondervan Publishing House. All rights reserved. Scripture quotations marked (TLB) are taken from *The Living Bible* copyright © 1971. Used by permission of Tyndale House Publishers, Inc., Wheaton, Illinois 60189. All rights reserved. Scripture quotations marked (MSG) are taken from *The Message*. Copyright © by Eugene H. Peterson 1993, 1994, 1995. Used by permission of NavPress Publishing Group. Scripture quotations marked (RSV) are taken from the *Revised Standard Version of the Bible,* copyright © 1946, 1952, and 1971 by the Division of Christian Education of the National Council of the Churches of Christ in the USA. Used by permission.

Names and facts from stories contained in this book have been changed, but the emotional and sexual struggles portrayed are true stories as related to the author through personal interviews, letters, or e-mails.

ISBN 1-57856-686-X

Copyright © 2003 by Shannon Ethridge

Published in association with the literary agency of Alive Communications, Inc., 7680 Goddard Street, Suite 200, Colorado Springs, CO 80920.

Printed in the United States of America
2003—First Edition

10 9 8 7 6 5 4 3 2 1

contents

foreword

(by Stephen Arterburn)

I am so grateful you have decided to go deeper and work through the concepts Shannon Ethridge presented in *Every Woman's Battle*. Completing the exercises in this workbook will strengthen your defenses in the battle to guard your heart. If you have personally struggled with disappointment, comparison, fantasy, lust, or unfaithfulness, I know you will find new insights as you take the time to study and implement the concepts in this workbook.

Studying this material on your own will help you cement new attitudes, thought patterns, and behaviors into your life. But Shannon and I desire something even greater for you; we want you to experience healing in your soul. God provides that healing through the company of other women who are determined to win their battles or who have fought and emerged victorious.

Though discussing your battle openly may sound frightening, I urge you not to isolate yourself from those who can help. Disconnection, cutting yourself off from others, is one of the most devastating consequences of every woman's battle. As the private world inside grows more potent, disconnection from God and close friends is the certain result. In contrast, God's plan for success involves each of us staying connected to Him and learning to connect even more deeply with others. James 5:16 reminds us to confess our sins to one another so we will experience healing. When we seek God's direction, He leads us back to relationship and openness with each other, where our healing can be fostered.

As you work through the material Shannon has provided, I hope you will strive to integrate all of your parts into a whole, complete, and authentic person. Most likely, as a result of the pain of every woman's battle, part of you has become fragmented, splitting off from the rest of you. What you believe has not been reflected in what you have been thinking and doing. Perhaps you, like many other women, dreamed of giving your heart to a man once and for all—forever—only to find your heart drifting away from him and toward someone else. Your private world may have become more powerful than your public world. Perhaps you have taken your secret desires and passions underground, out of sight, so that those close to you would never suspect. Now is the time to pull back the curtain on that internal life. Bring it out into the light and expose it for what it is: something less than God's best for you. Though you may receive moments of intense pleasure and connection, your thoughts and actions have, in reality, fragmented you from yourself, your God, and those around you. I hope this workbook will help you pick up the pieces and put the fragments back together.

One final thought as you move into this time of soul work. First Thessalonians 4:3 tells us, "It is God's will that you should be sanctified: that you should avoid sexual immorality." The standard of the world is far from sanctification. Even within the church many have abandoned the standards of God's Word, rationalizing their behavior as harmless. But God is calling you to a new standard—a standard of holiness and purity through obedience. Holiness requires more than a faithful body. It requires a pure heart, mind, and soul to be the woman God wants you to be. To be fully woman, you must be God's woman first and foremost. Just the fact that you hold this workbook in your hand is an indication that you truly do want to be God's woman.

As you complete your work here, I am praying that you will have new tools to live out your values consistently. That you will love truth—and its freedom—more than the lie of discontent. I pray that you will be focused on what you have rather than on what you do not have. I hope you will become grateful in whatever circumstances are before you. And I pray that you will be able to forgive, accept, and grow in your relationship with God, no matter what difficulties you are experiencing.

May God richly bless you as you pursue Him with a pure passion.

questions you may have about this workbook

What will the *Every Woman's Battle Workbook* do for me?
So often women read books and think of all the other people who need to hear its message. However, *Every Woman's Battle* is intended for every woman...especially you. This workbook will help you recognize your own unique struggle with sexual and emotional integrity and how God's plan for your fulfillment may differ from your own less effective plan.

You'll discover ways to guard not only your body, but also your mind, heart, and mouth against sexual compromise. Through thought-provoking questions and soul-searching exercises, you'll begin to see a new sexual revolution taking shape not just in the world, but inside of you.

Is this workbook enough, or do I also need the book *Every Woman's Battle*?
Although you will find excerpts throughout each chapter from the *Every Woman's Battle* book (each one marked at the beginning and end by this symbol: 📖), we recommend that you read along in the book to see the big picture and get the full effect of the concepts presented.

How much time is required? Do I need to work through every part of each chapter?

According to Annette, Dee, Jenny, Karen, and Lori (our gracious "guinea pigs" with this workbook), you should be able to finish each workbook chapter within twenty-five to thirty minutes. While it's important to work through all the questions in each chapter, you may want to spend more time on areas that target your specific needs.

Each chapter contains four parts: Planting Good Seeds (Personally Seeking God's Truth), Weeding Out Deception (Recognizing the Truth), Harvesting Fulfillment (Applying the Truth), and Growing Together (Sharing the Truth in Small-Group Discussion). The first three sections are intended for individual study. They will help you hide God's Word in your heart, recognize and remove things in your heart that hinder you in this battle, and reap the rewards of living a life of sexual and emotional integrity. The last section of each chapter is designed especially for group discussion, although it can also be done individually.

How do I organize a study group?

You'll be amazed at how much more you'll get out of this book and workbook if you go through it with a group of like-minded women. If you don't know of an existing group, start one of your own! Whether it's a Sunday-school class, a group of coworkers, neighbors, or friends, invite some women to review the book and workbook. Most will recognize that there is always room for improvement in the area of sexual and emotional integrity, and the book is designed to have something for every woman regardless of age, marital status, or previous sexual experience.

The time commitment for going through the book and workbook isn't significant. Most women can find an hour each week to read a chapter in the book and answer the corresponding questions in the workbook. In addition, your group will need to meet together twelve times to discuss each chapter, one at a time. Your meetings should be kept to a reasonable amount of time (I recommend sixty to ninety minutes) so everyone will consider it a blessing rather than a burden. If evenings are not a possibility, consider a weekly breakfast or brown-bag lunch meeting.

When women gather to discuss such an intimate topic, the temptation to rabbit-trail with a variety of other "safer" topics can be overwhelming, especially for someone who is uncomfortable at first. Therefore, one person should be designated as the group facilitator to ensure that the conversation stays on track. This facilitator has no responsibilities to teach, lecture, or prepare anything in advance, but simply to begin and end the meeting at the designated times and to make sure the conversation is moving along in a productive manner.

Before you begin meeting, consider allowing people time to invite friends of their own who may want to be a part of such a group. There is nothing more healing than several women coming together, removing masks they may have been hiding behind for years, and getting real with each other about the sexual and emotional issues that are common to all of us. If being so honest with a group of other women evokes feelings of fear and mistrust, I encourage you to turn to Myth 7 in chapter 3 of *Every Woman's Battle.* You are truly not alone in your struggles, and other women need to know that they are not alone, either. Will you be the one to tell them?

You never know, perhaps your group will rescue someone from the pit of inappropriate fantasies, the snare of masturbation, or perhaps you will start a group just before someone you know falls into an emotional or sexual affair. Your accountability group can truly be a lifeline not just for you, but for every woman who participates.

Take heart and know that our cries for help have been heard.
This book is a training manual that will help you avoid sexual
and emotional compromise and will show you how you can experience
God's plan for sexual and emotional fulfillment.
Do you want to be a woman of sexual and emotional integrity?
With God's help you can. Let's get started.

—from the introduction to *Every Woman's Battle*

not just a man's battle!

Read chapter 1 in *Every Woman's Battle*.

PLANTING GOOD SEEDS
(Personally Seeking God's Truth)

As you seek to discover God's plan for sexual and emotional fulfillment, these are some good seeds to plant in your heart:

> You have heard that it was said, "Do not commit adultery."
> But I tell you that anyone who looks at a [man longingly]
> has already committed adultery with [him] in [her] heart.
> (Matthew 5:27-28)

> Among you there must not be even a hint of sexual
> immorality. (Ephesians 5:3)

1. What do these verses say to you?

2. How does your life measure up to these standards?

For hope that you can win the battle for sexual and emotional integrity, a good seed to plant in your heart is 1 Corinthians 10:13:

> No temptation has seized you except what is common to [woman]. And God is faithful; he will not let you be tempted beyond what you can bear. But when you are tempted, he will also provide a way out so that you can stand up under it.

3. Rewrite this verse in your own words.

⚒ WEEDING OUT DECEPTION
(Recognizing the Truth)

> 📖 Over the past decade of pursuing my own healing from these (and other) issues, as well as teaching on the topic of sexual purity and restoration, I have come to understand that in some way or another sexual and emotional integrity is a battle that every woman fights.

Many believe that just because they are not involved in a physical, sexual affair they don't have a problem with sexual and emotional integrity. As a result, they engage in thoughts and behaviors that compromise their integrity and rob them of true sexual and emotional fulfillment. 📖

4. Do you agree with the statement that every woman fights the battle for sexual and emotional integrity? Why or why not?

5. Reflect back on the stories in the first chapter. Which one, if any, of these women's stories strikes a chord in you? How has reading her story opened your eyes to your own battle?

6. Circle how often you have engaged in any of the following:

Unhealthy Comparisons	Never	Sometimes	Often	Always
Mental Fantasies	Never	Sometimes	Often	Always
Emotional Affairs	Never	Sometimes	Often	Always
Romance Novels	Never	Sometimes	Often	Always
Soap Operas	Never	Sometimes	Often	Always
Masturbation	Never	Sometimes	Often	Always

Inappropriate Internet Activity	Never	Sometimes	Often	Always
Other Sexual Dysfunction(s)				
_____	Never	Sometimes	Often	Always
_____	Never	Sometimes	Often	Always

7. What areas of compromise do you need to weed out of your life?

8. Specifically, what effect has this activity had on your marriage? on your relationship with God? on your self-esteem?

🌾 HARVESTING FULFILLMENT
(Applying the Truth)

> 📖 I am thrilled to report that our marriage of thirteen years is still going strong and has never been better (although we, like any other couple, still have our moments). I'm thankful I never traded [Greg] in for another model, and even more thankful that he didn't give up on me, either. Together, we have discovered a new level of intimacy that we didn't know existed, all because I stopped comparing and criticizing and began embracing the uniqueness of my spouse. 📖

9. If you were to refrain from any of the compromising activities that you identified and (if you are married) began to focus all of your sexual energies on your husband, what would the result be in your marriage?

10. What would the result be in your relationship with God?

11. What would the result be on your self-esteem?

🍃 GROWING TOGETHER
(Sharing the Truth in Small-Group Discussion)

📖 When I hear people say that women don't struggle with sexual issues like men do, I cannot help but wonder what planet they are from or what rock they have been hiding under. Perhaps what they really mean is, the physical aspect of sexuality isn't an overwhelming temptation for women like it is for men.

Men and women struggle in different ways when it comes to sexual integrity. While a man's battle begins with what he takes in through his eyes, a woman's begins with her heart and her thoughts. A man must guard his eyes to maintain sexual integrity, but because God made women to be emotionally and mentally stimulated, we must closely guard our hearts and minds as well as our bodies if we want to experience God's plan for sexual and emotional fulfillment. A woman's battle is for sexual *and* emotional integrity. 📖

12. Why do you think so many people assume that women do not struggle with sexual issues?

13. What hinders women from recognizing sexual and emotional compromise?

14. Once women recognize it, what hinders us from talking about it with others?

📖 While a man needs mental, emotional, and spiritual connection, his physical needs tend to be in the driver's seat and his other needs ride along in the back. The reverse is true for women. If there is one particular need that drives us, it is certainly our emotional needs. That's why it's said that men *give love to get sex* and women *give sex to get love.* 📖

15. Have you ever given sex in order to get the love you were longing for? If so, did this method work for you? Why or why not?

16. What prompted you to read *Every Woman's Battle* and utilize this workbook?

17. Of the twenty-five questions asked to determine if you were engaged in a battle for sexual and emotional integrity (see page 15-17 in *Every Woman's Battle*), what surprised you? What scared you?

18. What particular question(s) hit home for you, and why?

19. What is the main thing you are hoping to gain over the next twelve weeks from:

    reading *Every Woman's Battle?*

    working through this workbook?

    participating in this discussion group?

❧

Lord, thank You that You are a faithful God who provides a way out whenever we are tempted. Thank You for revealing that we are not alone in our struggles for sexual and emotional integrity. As we seek to learn Your truths, weed deception out of our lives, harvest a bumper crop of fulfillment in our relationships, and grow together as sisters in Christ, we ask that You guide our hearts and minds into greater levels of personal holiness. In Jesus' name. Amen.

a new look
at sexual integrity

Read chapter 2 in *Every Woman's Battle*.

🪣 PLANTING GOOD SEEDS
(Personally Seeking God's Truth)

As you wonder if you can succeed at moving from a place of compromise to a place of sexual and emotional integrity, plant these good seeds in your heart:

> I, the LORD, have called you in righteousness;
>   I will take hold of your hand.
> I will keep you and will make you
>   to be a covenant for the people
>   and a light for the Gentiles,
> to open eyes that are blind,
>   to free captives from prison
>   and to release from the dungeon those
>   who sit in darkness.
>   (Isaiah 42:6-7)

> I can do everything God asks me to with the help of Christ
> who gives me the strength and power. (Philippians 4:13, TLB)

1. What effect does it have on your confidence level to know that God
   will hold your hand and lead you from darkness into light? Why?

To remind yourself about the most important things in life and in your
relationships, plant the following seed in your heart:

> Love the Lord your God with all your heart and with all
> your soul and with all your mind. This is the first and great-
> est commandment. And the second is like it: "Love your
> neighbor as yourself." All the Law and the Prophets hang
> on these two commandments. (Matthew 22:37)

2. How well has your life lined up with this verse? What changes do you
   need to make in order to fulfill these two commandments?

As you think about what kinds of behaviors you should or should not
engage in—including those not specifically forbidden in Scripture—plant
this seed in your heart:

"Everything is permissible"—but not everything is beneficial. "Everything is permissible"—but not everything is constructive. Nobody should seek [her] own good, but the good of others. (1 Corinthians 10:23-24)

3. Rewrite this verse in your own words.

🗙 WEEDING OUT DECEPTION
(Recognizing the Truth)

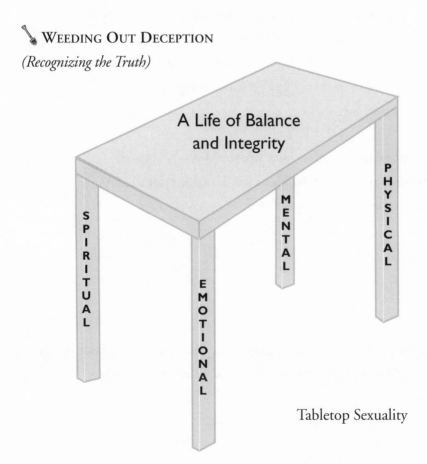

A Life of Balance
and Integrity

SPIRITUAL

EMOTIONAL

MENTAL

PHYSICAL

Tabletop Sexuality

📖 By definition, our sexuality isn't *what we do.* Even people who are committed to celibacy are sexual beings. Our sexuality is *who we are,* and we were made with a body, mind, heart, and spirit, not just a body. Therefore, sexual integrity is not just about physical chastity. It is about purity in all four aspects of our being (body, mind, heart, and spirit). When all four aspects line up perfectly, our "tabletop" (our life) reflects balance and integrity....

It's no laughing matter when one of the legs of our sexuality buckles, because then our lives can become a slippery slope leading to discontentment, sexual compromise, self-loathing, and emotional brokenness. When this happens, the blessing that God intended to bring richness and pleasure to our lives feels more like a curse that brings great pain and despair. 📖

4. In your dating relationships, where did you believe "the line" of sexual integrity to be? How far was it "okay" to go prior to marriage? Where did this belief come from?

5. If you ever crossed that imaginary line, were you able to back up and reestablish your preexisting standards? Why or why not?

6. As you read chapter 2, what insights did you gain about where the line between integrity and compromise should be located?

🌾 HARVESTING FULFILLMENT
(Applying the Truth)

> 📖 In order to have ultimate fulfillment and feel that physical, mental, emotional, and spiritual stability that God intended for us to have, we have to attend to each leg of our table according to God's perfect plan. If one leg is neglected, abused, or attended to in an unrighteous manner, the result is some sort of sexual compromise or emotional brokenness. When each leg is attended to or fulfilled righteously, the result is sexual integrity and emotional wholeness. 📖

7. In what ways are the following needs fulfilled in your life? Are any of these areas in need of attention? If so, how can you attend to these needs in a godly way?

Physical (sexual expression, exercise, proper nutrition):

Mental (educational or professional growth; a balance between stimulation and relaxation):

Emotional (quality time with spouse, family, or friends; enjoying a hobby):

Spiritual (connection with God through prayer, worship, Bible study; ministering to others):

❧ GROWING TOGETHER
(Sharing the Truth in Small-Group Discussion)

As someone in the group reads the following passage from *Every Woman's Battle* aloud, one sentence or phrase at a time, underline any phrases that you feel accurately describe you. Put a squiggly line under any phrases that stand out as being things you still need to strive toward.

📖 For a Christian woman, sexual and emotional integrity means that her thoughts, words, emotions, and actions all reflect an inner beauty and a sincere love for God, others, and for herself. This doesn't mean she is never tempted to think, say, feel, or do something inappropriate, but she tries diligently to resist these temptations and stands firm in her convictions. She doesn't use men in an attempt to get her emotional cravings met, or entertain sexual or romantic fantasies about men she is not married to. She doesn't compare her husband to other men, discounting his personal worth and withholding a part of herself from him as punishment for his imperfections. She doesn't dress to seek male attention, but she doesn't limit herself to a wardrobe of ankle-length muu-muus, either. She may dress fashionably and look sharp or may even appear sexy (like beauty, sexy is in the eye of the beholder), but her motivation isn't self-seeking or seductive. She presents herself as an attractive woman because she knows she represents God to others.

A woman of integrity lives a life that lines up with her Christian beliefs. She lives according to a standard of love rather than law. She does not claim to be a follower of Christ yet disregard His many teachings on sexual immorality, lustful thoughts, immodest dress, and inappropriate talk. A woman of integrity lives what she believes about God, and it shows everywhere from the boardroom to the bedroom. 📖

8. Share your conclusions (either with the entire group or in smaller groups) about what you see as your strengths and weaknesses when it comes to being a woman of sexual and emotional integrity.

∞

Jesus, thank You for giving us a new look at sexual integrity. Help us to live balanced, healthy lives as we seek to embrace, express, and control our sexuality according to Your perfect plan. In Your precious name we pray. Amen.

seven myths that intensify our struggle

Read chapter 3 in *Every Woman's Battle*.

🝆 PLANTING GOOD SEEDS
(Personally Seeking God's Truth)

As you seek to discern the difference between myth and truth in your battle for sexual and emotional integrity, the following verses hold good seeds to plant in your heart:

> Wisdom is better than weapons of war. (Ecclesiastes 9:18)

1. How can wisdom help you in your battle?

> It is God's will that you should be sanctified: that you should
> avoid sexual immorality; that each of you should learn to
> control [her] own body in a way that is holy and honorable,
> not in passionate lust like the heathen, who do not know
> God. (1 Thessalonians 4:3-5)

2. Do you believe that God can sanctify you and help you exercise control over your body? Why do you believe what you do? How would your relationships with men change if you learned to control your body in a way that is holy and honorable?

As you realize your need for God's grace in these matters, plant this in your heart:

> For we do not have a high priest who is unable to sympa-
> thize with our weaknesses, but we have one who has been
> tempted in every way, just as we are—yet was without sin.
> Let us then approach the throne of grace with confidence, so
> that we may receive mercy and find grace to help us in our
> time of need. (Hebrews 4:15-16)

3. How does it make you feel to know that Jesus can sympathize with your every weakness (even your sexual weaknesses)? Why?

☙ WEEDING OUT DECEPTION
(Recognizing the Truth)

📖 When we compare ourselves to others, we put one person above the other. We either come out on top (producing vanity and pride in our lives), or we come up short (producing feelings of disappointment with what God gave us). Regardless of how we measure up when we make these comparisons, our motives are selfish and sinful rather than loving. 📖

4. Have you compared yourself with other women or your husband to other men? In what ways? What has been the result?

📖 When you fantasize about someone else when making love with your husband, you are mentally making love with another man. *He,* not your husband, is the one you feel passionate about. *He,* not your husband, is the one you feel close to emotionally. 📖

5. Do you agree or disagree with the above statements? Why or why not?

6. Have you ever fantasized about another man while making love to your husband? How did this affect your ultimate fulfillment?

📖 "If sin doesn't know you, it won't call your name!" Once the sin of masturbation does know you by name, it *will* call. And call…and call…and call…. The only way to kill a bad habit is to *starve it to death.* Starving a bad habit can be painful, but not as painful as letting it rule over you. 📖

7. If masturbation has been an issue for you, what benefit have you believed it would bring? What effect has masturbation had on your thought life and on your ability to control your body in relationships with men?

🐚 HARVESTING FULFILLMENT
(Applying the Truth)

📖 God gives us grace to accept our husbands and ourselves as we really are, and He gives us the ability to truly love one another unconditionally and unreservedly.

If we crave genuine intimacy, we must learn to seek it only in this kind of grace-filled relationship. The word *intimacy* itself can best be defined by breaking it into syllables: *in-to-me-see.* Can we see into one another and respect, appreciate, and value what is really there, regardless of how that measures up to anyone else? That is what unconditional love and relational intimacy is all about, and this type of intimacy can be discovered only by two people who are seeking sexual and emotional integrity with all their mind, body, heart, and soul. 📖

8. Do you have any reservations about your husband (or those closest to you) seeing into every part of you? Why or why not? What, if anything, do you hide from your husband (or those closest to you)— and why?

9. As intimacy blossoms in your marriage and you see into your husband's heart and mind, how can you give him the same grace that God gives to you? What things about him might you need to accept in order to love him unconditionally and unreservedly?

📖 Put all your eggs in one basket. Invest in the relationship you've got. Focus on your marriage wholeheartedly, as if no other man existed. Assume that your spouse is the man you will grow old with. Your husband is God's gift to you. Unwrap the gift and enjoy him for as long as you have him. 📖

10. In order for you to invest all that you've got into your marriage relationship, what needs to change? How will this affect your relationship with your husband? How will this, in turn, affect your level of fulfillment?

❧ GROWING TOGETHER
(Sharing the Truth in Small-Group Discussion)

📖 Sixty-seven percent of all women will experience at least one or more premarital or extramarital affair in her lifetime.[1] That is the number of women who *give in* to these temptations. I believe the percentage is much higher (I'm guessing in the 90 percent range) of those women who simply experience the temptation to engage in premarital or extramarital affairs. 📖

---

1. Tim Clinton, from a class titled "Counselor Professional Identity, Function and Ethics Videotape Course," External Degree Program, Liberty University, Lynchburg, Va. Used with permission.

11. Did you find this statistic surprising? Why or why not?

12. Which of the seven myths discussed in chapter 3 are ones that you have previously bought into? How has this intensified your struggle?

13. As you read about these myths, did God speak to you about an issue that is currently keeping you from discovering His plan for your sexual and emotional fulfillment? What did you feel God was revealing to you, and why?

14. What are you doing to incorporate this truth into your daily life?

15. Do you have someone you could ask to help hold you accountable in your battle for sexual and emotional integrity? Are you willing to be held accountable in this area? Why or why not?

∞

*F*ather God, thank You for giving us Your truth and dispelling the myths that cloud our judgment. We acknowledge that all wisdom comes from You and that Your truth is all we need to set us free to enjoy healthy relationships. In Your Son's name we pray. Amen.

time for a new revolution

Read chapter 4 in *Every Woman's Battle*.

🪣 PLANTING GOOD SEEDS
(Personally Seeking God's Truth)

As you seek to become the person that God designed you to be, a good seed to plant in your heart is:

> [God] is looking for those with changed hearts and minds.
> Whoever has that kind of change in [her] life will get [her]
> praise from God. (Romans 2:29, TLB)

1. How has your life conformed to worldly patterns? How do your heart and mind need to be changed in order to avoid conforming to such patterns any longer?

As you reclaim God's gift of authority over Satan and the world and exercise self-control, a good seed to plant in your heart is Galatians 5:22-23:

> But the fruit of the Spirit is love, joy, peace, patience, kindness, goodness, faithfulness, gentleness and self-control.

2. Which fruit of the Spirit do you feel is evident in your life? Which are in need of further development and why?

3. As you seek to fully understand who God made you to be, some good seeds to plant in your heart are the scriptures listed in the "Who I Am in Christ" chart at the close of chapter 4 (page 61-63). Which of these scriptures stand out to you as having the power to transform your life if you embraced them and lived accordingly?

(Remember that the thirty-day challenge of reciting these scriptures daily will help you internalize who you are in Christ).

⚊ WEEDING OUT DECEPTION
(Recognizing the Truth)

> 📖 I was seeking to understand why I still felt tempted out-
> side of my marriage, so my therapist asked me to spend a
> week making a list of every man I had ever been with sexu-
> ally or had pursued emotionally. I was shocked and saddened
> to see how long my list had grown through the years.
>
> At the next visit, she asked me to spend a week praying
> and asking myself, "What do each of these men have in
> common?" God showed me that each relationship had
> been with someone who was older than I and in some form
> of authority over me—my professor, my boss, my lawyer.
>
> As I searched my soul to discern why such a common
> thread existed in my relational pursuits, the root of the issue
> became evident: my hunger for power over a man. 📖

4. If you were to create a list of the men you have had sexual experiences
   with, pursued emotionally (or allowed to pursue you), or fantasized
   about, what common threads do you think would surface? (If it would
   help to make a list, do so on a separate sheet of paper that can be
   destroyed later.)

5. What have you hoped to gain from previous sexual relationships,
   emotional entanglements, or inappropriate fantasies (power, status,

excitement, distraction from boredom or pressure, attention, affirma-
tion, affection, security, and so on)?

6. What do you suspect may be the root issue that has driven you toward
such behavior?

7. Do you believe that what you are looking for can truly be found in an
unhealthy relationship or in fantasy? If so, have you found it? If not,
where would be a better place to look?

🐚 HARVESTING FULFILLMENT
(Applying the Truth)

> 📖 In my attempts to fill the father-shaped hole in my heart
> and establish some semblance of self-worth through these
> dysfunctional relationships, I was creating a long list of
> shameful liaisons and a trunk load of emotional baggage. I
> was overlooking the only true source of satisfaction and self-

worth: an intimate relationship with my heavenly Father.
Through pursuing this relationship first and foremost, not
only has Jesus become my first love and given me a sense of
worth beyond what any man could give, He has also restored
my relationship with my earthly father and helped me
remain faithful to my husband. 📖

8. Do you believe that you can have an intimate and satisfying relationship with God? Why or why not? What are you currently doing to
pursue this kind of relationship with God?

9. What would be the result if every woman on the planet discovered
God's plan for sexual and emotional fulfillment and lived accordingly?

10. Do you believe that God truly desires sexual and emotional fulfillment
for your life? for every woman's life? Write your response in the form
of a prayer, asking God for this fulfillment for you and for every other
woman (or asking for faith to believe it is possible).

❧ GROWING TOGETHER
(Sharing the Truth in Small-Group Discussion)

11. What is the most beneficial nugget of wisdom that you gleaned from this chapter? Why?

> 📖 Rather than use what beauty God had given me to bring glory to Him, I used it as bait to lure men into feeding my ego. Rather than inspiring men to worship God, I subconsciously wanted them to worship me, and if I was successful in hooking a man with my charms, I felt secretly powerful. 📖

12. What do you feel is the reason that God gives physical assets to a woman (an attractive body, a lovely face, beautiful eyes, a brilliant smile, or a magnetic personality)? What responsibilities come along with these gifts? How should we use these gifts? How should we not use them?

13. Do you use the physical assets that God gave you to glorify *yourself* rather than Him? Explain your answer.

📖 Turning the tide in our culture may seem like an impossible task, but we are not alone in this challenge. *God* will turn the tide *through* us. He simply asks us to submit our own lives to Him and to be a witness to what His power and love can do. As more and more women receive this revelation and share this wisdom with others, the tide will eventually turn on its own. We need to begin by focusing on our own behaviors so that we no longer allow the world to influence us. This can only be done by personally reclaiming the gift of authority that Eve originally gave away. 📖

14. If you believe it is time for a new revolution, what specifically can you do in order to:

exercise your God-given authority and seek to understand who you are in Christ?

embrace God's plan for sexual and emotional fulfillment?

keep the world from leading you back into compromise?

inspire other women to pursue sexual and emotional integrity?

Heavenly Father, we acknowledge that our society has strayed far from Your plan for sexual and emotional fulfillment. It is truly time for a new sexual revolution, and we pray that it would begin today in each of us. In Jesus' name. Amen.

taking thoughts captive

Read chapter 5 in *Every Woman's Battle*.

⚘ PLANTING GOOD SEEDS
(Personally Seeking God's Truth)

As you recognize that the battle for sexual and emotional integrity begins in the mind, a good seed to plant in your heart is 2 Corinthians 10:3-5:

> For though we live in the world, we do not wage war as the
> world does. The weapons we fight with are not the weapons
> of the world.... We take captive every thought to make it
> obedient to Christ.

1. How is taking thoughts captive a weapon against sexual and emotional compromise? Is it a weapon you've learned to use effectively? Why or why not?

As you are tempted to pursue sexual and emotional fulfillment the world's way, Romans 12:1-2 is a good seed to plant in your heart:

> Therefore, I urge you, [sisters], in view of God's mercy, to offer your bodies as living sacrifices, holy and pleasing to God—this is your spiritual act of worship. Do not conform any longer to the pattern of this world, but be transformed by the renewing of your mind. Then you will be able to test and approve what God's will is—his good, pleasing and perfect will.

2. Using your own words, describe what Paul was saying in each of his three sentences above:

   a)

   b)

   c)

⚒ WEEDING OUT DECEPTION
(Recognizing the Truth)

📖 In the movie *What Women Want,* Nick Marshall (Mel Gibson) develops a telepathic ability to hear each thought, opinion, and desire that goes through every woman's head.

Imagine this: Tomorrow morning you wake up and every man on the planet has developed the ability to read your mind just by being in your presence. Does the thought make you nervous?…

Even though we can rest assured that men and women aren't likely to develop this sensitivity anytime soon, we have an even bigger concern. God has had this ability all along. Could you, like David, be so bold as to pray such a thing as this: "Test me, O LORD, and try me, examine my heart and my mind" (Psalm 26:2)? 📖

3. How does it make you feel to know that God is fully aware of your each and every thought? What effect do the inappropriate thoughts we entertain have on God's heart? Why?

4. Are you, like David, *eager* for the Holy Spirit to examine your mind and test your thoughts? Why or why not?

Consider the following verse:

> I am jealous for you with a godly jealousy. I promised you to
> one husband, to Christ, so that I might present you as a pure
> virgin to him. But I am afraid that just as Eve was deceived
> by the serpent's cunning, your minds may somehow be led
> astray from your sincere and pure devotion to Christ.
> (2 Corinthians 11:2-3)

5. How consistent have you been in your devotion to Christ? What
   things keep your mind from being fully devoted to Him?

6. What specific things can you do to restore your devotion to Christ?
   What effect will this have on your thought life? on your ability to resist
   temptation?

🐚 HARVESTING FULFILLMENT
(Applying the Truth)

> Sow a thought, reap an action:
> Sow an action, reap a habit;
> Sow a habit, reap a character;
> Sow a character, reap a destiny.
> —Samuel Smiles

7. What specific things do you feel that God designed you to accomplish in life? What roles do you want to be fondly remembered for at the end of your life?

8. Describe the character traits of such a person who accomplished these things or fulfilled these roles you listed.

9. What regular actions and habits would a person of such character practice?

10. Does your thought life equip you or hinder you from being the person God designed you to be and from fulfilling the destiny that He has for you? How so?

11. What specific recurring thoughts do you need to take captive in order for you to be all that God made you to be? Are you willing to surrender those and make them obedient to Christ?

🌿 GROWING TOGETHER

(Sharing the Truth in Small-Group Discussion)

12. What in this chapter was most helpful to you? Why?

13. What new line of defense do you plan to incorporate into your life in order to:

resist temptation at the gate?

redirect tempting thoughts?

renew your mind?

14. What does the following saying mean to you? How would you explain it to a younger woman?

You *can't* keep a bird from flying over your head, but you *can* keep him from building a nest in your hair!

15. How do you keep "birds" from "building a nest in your hair?" In other words, how do you distract yourself in order to avoid entertaining random, inappropriate thoughts?

📖 We are rehearsing when we think about the conversations we would have with a particular man if we were ever alone with him, when we entertain thoughts of an intimate rendezvous, or wish that a certain man would take special notice of us…. Then when Satan lays the trap and leads that man in your direction, guess what? We are more than likely going to play the part exactly the way we have rehearsed it. When we don't guard our minds in our relationships with men, we weaken our resistance before any encounter takes place. 📖

16. Do you agree that our thoughts are often rehearsals for how we behave in the face of temptation? Why or why not?

17. Share with the group an example of how you either succumbed to or resisted temptation because of how you rehearsed your part in your thoughts. What did you learn from this experience?

∞

*H*oly Spirit, search our minds and reveal those thoughts hindering our ultimate fulfillment in relationships with others and with You. Continue to teach us to take every thought captive and make it obedient to Christ. In Jesus' name. Amen.

guarding your heart

Read chapter 6 in *Every Woman's Battle*.

🌱 PLANTING GOOD SEEDS
(Personally Seeking God's Truth)

As you seek to understand the pivotal role that your heart plays in your sexual, emotional, and spiritual life, some good seeds to plant in your heart include:

> Above all else, guard your heart,
>> for it is the wellspring of life.
>>> (Proverbs 4:23)

> I the LORD search the heart
>> and examine the mind,
> to reward a [woman] according to [her] conduct,
>> according to what [her] deeds deserve.
>>> (Jeremiah 17:10)

1. According to these passages, why should you guard your heart?

As you seek to align your life with God's plan for sexual and emotional fulfillment, a good seed to plant in your heart is:

> You know the next commandment pretty well, too: "Don't
> go to bed with another's spouse." But don't think you've pre-
> served your virtue simply by staying out of bed. Your *heart*
> can be corrupted by lust even quicker than your *body*.
> (Matthew 5:27, MSG)

2. What do you think Jesus was saying to His disciples in this passage? What does the passage say to you personally?

⚒ WEEDING OUT DECEPTION
(Recognizing the Truth)

> 📖 While the need to love and to feel loved is a universal cry
> of the heart, the problem lies in where we look for this love.
> If we are not getting the love we need or want from a man—
> whether or not we have a husband—we may go searching
> for it. Some look in bars and others in business offices. Some
> look on college campuses and some look in churches. Some
> women look to male friends while others look to fantasy.
> When love eludes them, some women seek to medicate the
> pain of loneliness or rejection. Some take solace in food;
> others in sexual relationships with any willing partner. Some

turn to soap operas; others to shopping; and still others to self-gratification.

If you have tried any of these avenues for long, you have likely come to a dead end. Your pursuit has left you longing for something greater, something deeper, something more. 📖

3. Have you looked for love in problematic places? If so, where did you look, and what was the result?

4. How have you sought to medicate the pain of loneliness or rejection? How has this worked for you?

📖 Rather than running to the Ultimate Healer for relief from our emotional wounds, women often make idols of relationships—worshiping a man instead of God. We begin submitting to a man's and our own unholy desires rather than submitting to God's desires for our holiness and purity, thus becoming a slave to our passions.

When we peel back the layers of this issue, we can see the core problem: *doubt that God can truly satisfy our innermost needs.* So we look to a man who is not our husband and eventually discover that he doesn't "fix" us, either. 📖

5. Do you believe that at the core of sexual and emotional compromise is *doubt* that God is truly sufficient to satisfy our innermost needs? Why or why not?

6. Do *you* doubt that God can meet *your* deepest needs? If so, write a prayer to God confessing this doubt and asking Him to remove it. If not, write a prayer affirming your belief that He is sufficient.

📖 [God] wants to dwell in every part of your heart, not just rent a room there. He wants to fill your heart to overflowing.

Don't let guilt from past mistakes keep you from seeking this truly satisfying first-love relationship with Him. God does not despise you for the way you've tried to fill the void in your heart. He says, "Come now, let us reason together.... Though your sins are like scarlet, they shall be white as snow; though they are red as crimson, they shall be like wool" (Isaiah 1:18). He is eager to cleanse your heart and teach you how to guard it from future pain and loneliness. 📖

7. Does God dwell in your heart or just rent a room there? Does a guilty heart hinder you from experiencing the fullness of God's unconditional love for you? Why or why not?

🌽 HARVESTING FULFILLMENT
(Applying the Truth)

8. In your own words, explain the stages of the green-light level of emotional connection and why these are acceptable. (Please reference the illustration on the next page.)

Attraction

Attention

FOR SINGLE WOMEN   FOR MARRIED WOMEN

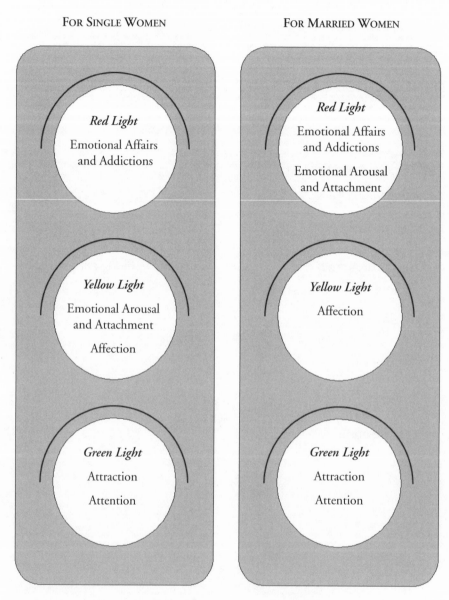

Identifying Green, Yellow, and Red Levels of Emotional Connection

9. In your own words, explain the stages of the yellow-light level of emotional connection and why we need to exercise caution with these stages.

   Emotional Arousal and Attachment (single women only)

   Affection

10. Finally, explain the stages of the red-light level and why we need to stop before crossing these lines.

    Emotional Affairs and Addictions

    Emotional Arousal and Attachment (married women only)

📖 As you use caution and strive to refrain from red-light stages of emotional connection, you will regain the self-control, dignity, and self-respect you may have lost if you have compromised your sexual integrity. You can also expect a renewed sense of connection and intimacy with your husband and purity in your friendships or work relationships with other men. But best of all, when God looks on your pure heart and sees that you are guarding it against unhealthy relationships, He will reward you with an even greater revelation of Himself. 📖

11. What gives you the most incentive for avoiding the red-light stages of emotional connection? What specifically can you do to avoid crossing the line between integrity and compromise?

🌱 GROWING TOGETHER

(Sharing the Truth in Small-Group Discussion)

12. What was the most beneficial thing you learned in chapter 6 about guarding your heart? Why was this helpful to you?

13. How would your life have been different had you learned about guarding your heart before you started dating?

14. If (or when) you have children, how can you share with them the concepts about guarding your heart that would have benefited you as a teenager?

Consider the following passage from *Every Woman's Battle,* then break into smaller groups and answer the questions adapted from the close of chapter 6.

> 📖 While avoiding unhealthy emotional connections and relationships is important, it's not enough to guarantee success in keeping our hearts guarded against compromise. The secret to ultimate emotional satisfaction is to pursue a mad, passionate love relationship with the One who made our hearts, the One who purifies our hearts, and the One who strengthens our hearts against worldly temptations. The secret is to focus your heart on your First Love. 📖

15. Have I *really* invested much time getting to know God personally and intimately? What have I done to get to know God?

16. Have I given God as many chances as I have given other men? fantasy? Internet chat rooms?

17. Am I willing to make the choice to pray or to dance to worship music or to go for a walk with God instead of picking up the phone to call a guy when I am lonely?

18. Am I willing to invite God to satisfy my every need by letting go of all the things, people, and thoughts that I use to medicate my pain, fear, or loneliness so that I might become totally dependent upon Him?

19. After answering these questions, can you honestly say that Jesus Christ is truly your first love? If not, what can you do to enhance the intimacy in your relationship with Him?

∞

Create in me a pure heart, O God, and renew a steadfast spirit within me. Do not cast me from your presence or take your Holy Spirit from me. Restore to me the joy of your salvation and grant me a willing spirit, to sustain me. Then I will teach transgressors your ways, and sinners will turn back to you (prayer of David, Psalm 51:10-13).

locking loose lips

Read chapter 7 in *Every Woman's Battle*.

PLANTING GOOD SEEDS
(Personally Seeking God's Truth)

As you consider the effect of your words on your relationship with God, with others, and with yourself, some good seeds to plant in your heart are:

> If anyone considers [herself] religious and yet does not keep a tight rein on [her] tongue, [she] deceives [herself] and [her] religion is worthless. (James 1:26)

> The tongue is a small part of the body, but it makes great boasts. Consider what a great forest is set on fire by a small spark. The tongue is also a fire, a world of evil among the parts of the body. It corrupts the whole person, sets the whole course of his life on fire. (James 3:5-6)

1. What do these verses say to you?

As you seek to integrate your words with your life of sexual and emotional integrity, plant these seeds in your heart:

> For out of the overflow of the heart the mouth speaks. The good [woman] brings good things out of the good stored up in [her], and the evil [woman] brings evil things out of the evil stored up in [her]. But I tell you that [women] will have to give account on the day of judgment for every careless word they have spoken. For by your words you will be acquitted, and by your words you will be condemned. (Matthew 12:34-37)

> But among you there must not be even a hint of sexual immorality, or of any kind of impurity…because these are improper for God's holy people. Nor should there be obscenity, foolish talk or course joking which are out of place, but rather thanksgiving. (Ephesians 5:3-4)

2. Do you agree that the words that flow from your mouth are actually a reflection of what is in your heart? Why or why not?

☙ WEEDING OUT DECEPTION
(Recognizing the Truth)

📖 What is a four-letter word for a woman's favorite foreplay activity? T-A-L-K!

Think about it. What affair has ever taken place without intimate words exchanged? Women often tell me, "I've not been unfaithful to my husband. All this man and I have done is talk." 📖

3. Do you feel that a man or woman can be unfaithful simply because of the words they exchange with a person other than his or her spouse? Why or why not?

📖 While it may be okay to act amorously (as if desiring romance) toward someone you are interested in developing a mutually beneficial relationship with, flirting is a different matter. Flirting could also be called "teasing," as the person doing the flirting has no serious intent. 📖

4. Do you think it is okay for a woman—even a single woman—to flirt with a man if she has no intention of investing in a romantic relationship? Explain your answer.

5. If you enjoy flirting with men, what do you think you might be looking to gain? Has flirting ever put you in an uncomfortable or compromising situation? Explain your answer.

> 📖 Women can be far too nurturing in situations, even
> when red flags begin to surface. We often think, *But he*
> *needs me… I'm just trying to be a friend… How can I possi-*
> *bly* not *help? That would not be very Christianlike!* 📖

6. Do you tend to be overly nurturing with men, frequently playing
   the "mother" or "counselor" or "best friend" role? If so, what may
   be behind this tendency?

7. Have you experienced temptations to compromise your sexual and
   emotional integrity because you were being "too good for your own
   good?" If so, how can you overcome this tendency?

🐚 Harvesting Fulfillment
(Applying the Truth)

> 📖 If we long to be women of sexual and emotional in-
> tegrity, we must understand what a mighty weapon our
> words are. Words are what will lead us into an affair, or
> words will stop an affair before it ever begins. 📖

8. Do you agree that a woman can either start or avoid an affair simply by the words she allows to come out of her mouth? Why or
why not?

9. Suppose a friend tells you, "I don't want to fall into an affair, but
I feel I must be honest with this man about my feelings for him."
How would you respond? Does being a woman of integrity mean
that we must always be open and honest about our feelings with
the object of our temptation? Why or why not?

10. Let's suppose that you have feelings for a particular man, but you
refuse to act on them or confess them to anyone other than God and
an accountability partner. How do you think that would make you

feel to display such strength in the face of temptation? How might you benefit from this choice spiritually and emotionally?

📖 In our quest for relational intimacy, remember that there is Someone we can whisper our heart's desires to and get our boosts from who isn't going to jeopardize our integrity but will strengthen it.

If you are thinking, *No way will talking to God ever excite me like talking to a man will,* then you haven't allowed yourself to be courted by our Creator. The same God whose words possessed the power to form the entire universe longs to whisper words into your hungry heart that have the power to thrill you, heal you, and draw you into a deeper love relationship than you ever imagined possible. A guy may say that you look fine, but God's Word says, "The king is enthralled by your beauty" (Psalm 45:11). A man may tell you, "Of course I love you," but God says, "I have loved you with an everlasting love; I have drawn you with loving-kindness" (Jeremiah 31:3). Even your husband may tell you, "I'm committed to you until death," but God says, "Never will I leave you; never will I forsake you." (Hebrews 13:5) 📖

11. If you have experienced such affirmations from God, how can they sustain you in times of emotional longing outside of marriage? Or if

you have never experienced such intimacy and ecstasy in your relationship with God, how might you cultivate that?

🌿 GROWING TOGETHER
(Sharing the Truth in Small-Group Discussion)

12. What were the most valuable lessons you took from this chapter? How
    can you hold on to them and draw from them in times of temptation?

📖 It has been said that men use conversation as a means of
communicating information, but women use conversation as
a means of bonding. While communicating and bonding
with our spouses, children, or female friends is great, communicating and bonding with men outside our marriage or
with men we wouldn't choose to date is dangerous and often
destructive. And yes, the more we communicate with a person, the more we bond, so we would do well to take a lesson
from the men in this area and learn to stick to business a
little better. We can learn to communicate with men in
friendly but to-the-point ways that will not jeopardize our
emotional integrity. 📖

13. Have you ever bonded with a man unintentionally due to excess communication? What did you learn from this experience?

14. What boundaries have you implemented (or may need to implement) to keep from bonding with men in inappropriate ways, whether in person, over the phone, or in cyberspace?

15. If you never exchange inappropriate words with a man (in person, over the phone, or in cyberspace), what is the likelihood that you will fall into a sexual affair?

16. How does it make you feel to know that resisting an emotional or sexual affair may be as easy as choosing appropriate words and avoiding inappropriate words? Is this revelation a relief to you? Why or why not?

∞

Lord, impress upon us the magnitude of the power that our words possess. We ask You to sanctify our speech at all times and with all people. Teach us to use our words to draw attention to You rather than to ourselves. Help us to speak blessings into other people's lives and to listen carefully as You speak blessings over us. In Jesus' name. Amen.

building better boundaries

Read chapter 8 in *Every Woman's Battle*.

🌱 PLANTING GOOD SEEDS
(Personally Seeking God's Truth)

As you seek to evaluate what weak links may exist in your armor of protection against sexual and emotional compromise, a good seed to plant in your heart is 1 Corinthians 6:19-20:

> Do you not know that your body is a temple of the Holy
> Spirit, who is in you, whom you have received from God?
> You are not your own; you were bought at a price. There-
> fore honor God with your body.

1. What did Paul mean when he said our bodies are a "temple of the Holy Spirit"? How might this concept change a woman's view of her sexual conduct? How can we honor God with our bodies?

As you consider whether your personal boundaries may need to be strengthened, plant Galatians 6:7-8 in your heart:

> Do not be deceived: God cannot be mocked. A [woman]
> reaps what [she] sows. The one who sows to please [her]
> sinful nature, from that nature will reap destruction; the
> one who sows to please the Spirit, from the Spirit will
> reap eternal life.

2. Based on the sexual or relational seeds you are currently sowing, what can you expect to reap? Explain your answer.

As you seek to believe that your ultimate value comes from your attitude toward God rather than your appearance, some good seeds to plant in your heart are in these verses:

> I also want women to dress modestly, with decency and pro-
> priety, not with braided hair or gold or pearls or expensive
> clothes, but with good deeds, appropriate for women who
> profess to worship God. (1 Timothy 2:9-10)

> Charm is deceptive, and beauty is fleeting;
>   but a woman who fears the LORD is to be praised.
> Give her the reward she has earned,
>   and let her works bring her praise at the city gate.
>   (Proverbs 31:30-31)

3. What do you think it means to fear the Lord? How might a woman benefit from becoming a woman who fears the Lord?

4. Why do you think women often fear other people's opinion of their appearance more than they fear God's opinion of their hearts? Which of these describes you? How do you think a woman can change her focus from being concerned about how she looks to being more concerned with the condition of her heart?

WEEDING OUT DECEPTION
(Recognizing the Truth)

> 📖 While the Bible doesn't specifically state how long a skirt should be or what sections of skin should always be covered, we can always go back to Jesus' commandment as a guideline for how we are to dress: Love your neighbor as yourself. 📖

5. Are you prone to dress for attention rather than to dress for respect? Why or why not?

6. Close your eyes and imagine standing in front of your closet. What clothes do you have that are likely to tempt a man to lust after your body? Are you willing to sacrifice the ego boost you may get from wearing those clothes for the sake of loving your neighbor?

📖 The only way to truly protect yourself is to guard against sexual compromise altogether. No condom fully protects you against the physical consequences of sexually immoral behavior. Even more important, no condom protects you against the spiritual consequences of sin (broken fellowship with God). No condom will protect you from the emotional consequences of a broken heart. Therefore, don't think in terms of "safe sex," but in terms of "saving sex" until marriage or remarriage. Wise is the woman who avoids compromising behavior that can put her body at risk of disease. 📖

7. Have you jeopardized your sexual integrity because you believed that using a condom during intercourse constitutes "safe sex"? Why do some people make the assumption that as long as a woman doesn't get pregnant or contract a disease that sex outside of marriage is okay?

8. Even if a woman escapes the physical consequences of premarital sex, what emotional and spiritual consequences may she face?

HARVESTING FULFILLMENT
(Applying the Truth)

📖 You have probably heard gourmet chefs on the cooking channel say that when it comes to food, presentation is everything. Presentation *is* everything, not just with food, but also with your body. One of the concepts that I impress upon women is that we teach people how to treat us. We either teach them to treat us with respect or we teach them to treat us with disrespect. 📖

9. Do you agree that the way a woman dresses affects whether others treat her with respect or disrespect? Explain your answer.

10. Has reading *Every Woman's Battle* raised any convictions within you about changing the way you present yourself with a certain person or in a certain setting? Explain your answer.

    📖 When you spend time with someone, you are giving that person a gift: *your presence.* It's true. The gift of your company is very precious and of value beyond description. Underneath your breasts lies a beating heart where the Holy Spirit makes His home. Behind your face is a brain that possesses the mind of Christ. Be wary of men who are intrigued by the wrapping but fail to see the value of what is inside the package. They may want to play with the bow…untie the ribbon…peek through the wrapping. 📖

11. Do you consider your presence a gift to those with whom you choose to spend your time? Why or why not?

12. If you felt that you were appreciated more for your heart, mind, and spirit than for your "outer wrapping," how might it change how you feel about yourself?

13. How can you strengthen your emphasis on the "inner package" so that your beauty radiates from within?

❧ GROWING TOGETHER
(Sharing the Truth in Small-Group Discussion)

> 📖 Your body is the temple of the Holy Spirit; your heart,
> God's dwelling place. As a believer, you have the mind of
> Christ. And your words are instruments of His wisdom and
> encouragement to others. When you put on the full armor
> of God and vigilantly guard your body, heart, mind, and
> mouth without compromise, you are well on your way to
> reaping the physical, emotional, mental, and spiritual bene-
> fits of sexual integrity. 📖

14. Do you wholeheartedly believe that your body is a temple of the Holy Spirit? that your heart is God's dwelling place? that you have the mind of Christ? that your words are God's instrument of wisdom and encouragement to others? Why or why not?

15. If you were to embrace these truths, believing each of them to be your birthright as a believer in Christ, what effect would it have on your self-esteem? on your relationships?

16. As a result of reading the past four chapters in the part of *Every Woman's Battle* titled "Designing a New Defense," what new ways have you learned to guard your body, heart, mind, and mouth against compromise?

17. What do you believe the physical, emotional, mental, and spiritual benefits of sexual integrity to be? What benefits are you already enjoying? What benefits do you hope to gain?

⊗

*F*ather God, where would we be were it not for Your divine protection? Thank you for teaching us appropriate physical and relational boundaries so that we may guard the temple of Your Holy Spirit. Continue to instill in each of us a sense of modesty and propriety so that we can reflect Your glorious image to all we encounter. In Jesus' holy and precious name. Amen.

sweet surrender

Read chapter 9 in *Every Woman's Battle*.

🌱 PLANTING GOOD SEEDS
(Personally Seeking God's Truth)

As you let go of past emotional pain and seek to reconcile relationships, a good seed to plant in your heart is James 3:17-18:

> But the wisdom that comes from heaven is first of all pure;
> then peace-loving, considerate, submissive, full of mercy and
> good fruit, impartial and sincere. Peacemakers who sow in
> peace raise a harvest of righteousness.

1. What do you think it means to "sow in peace"? How does an unwillingness to forgive affect one's life? marriage? fulfillment?

As you surrender your pride, embrace humility, and recognize that nothing short of God's grace will help you overcome sexual temptations, a good seed to plant in your heart is Titus 2:11:

> For the grace of God that brings salvation has appeared to
> all [women]. It teaches us to say "No" to ungodliness and
> worldly passions, and to live self-controlled, upright and
> godly lives in this present age, while we wait for the blessed
> hope—the glorious appearing of our great God and Savior,
> Jesus Christ, who gave himself for us to redeem us from all
> wickedness and to purify for himself a people that are his
> very own, eager to do what is good.

2. Do you believe that God's grace to resist sexual sin is available to anyone who believes in Christ? Why or why not?

3. Are you eager to live a self-controlled, upright, and godly life? Do you feel that God's grace is sufficient for you to live such a life? Why or why not?

WEEDING OUT DECEPTION
(Recognizing the Truth)

 📖 If you want to win the battle for sexual integrity, you must let go of past emotional pain. Maybe a father who was absent, either emotionally or physically, wounded you. Maybe the distance in your relationship with your mother left you feeling desperately lonely. Perhaps your siblings or friends never treated you with dignity or respect. If you were abused in any way (physically, sexually, or verbally) as a child, maybe you have anger and pain that has yet to be reconciled.

 Perhaps old lovers took advantage of your vulnerabilities, strung you along, or were unfaithful to you. Or maybe you've never understood why God allowed ——— to happen (you fill in the blank). Regardless of its source, we must surrender the pain from our past in order to stand strong in the battle for sexual and emotional integrity. 📖

Use the chart on the next page to process some of the past emotional pain you have experienced that has possibly left you vulnerable to sexual and/or emotional compromise. If you have more than one relationship to reconcile in this way, you may reproduce this chart.

HARVESTING FULFILLMENT
(Applying the Truth)

 📖 Why is [fear] such a hindrance? Because *fear* is the opposite of faith.... How can we focus on what we know God will do when we think we are doomed? Such lack of faith

Who is the person who caused my past emotional pain? How?	
How did this make me feel?	
How did this event/relationship make me vulnerable to temptation?	
How does this still affect me?	
What personal pain may have caused this person to hurt me?	
How does my unforgiveness affect this person?	
How does my unforgiveness affect me and my loved ones?	
How would my forgiveness affect this person?	
How would my forgiveness affect me and my loved ones?	
Can I cancel this debt as Jesus canceled mine? Why or why not?	
How can I pray for this person?	
How can I avoid causing this same pain in others' lives?	

says to God, "Even though you've carried me this far, you are probably going to fail me now, aren't you?"…

The same is true in our battle against sexual and emotional compromise. Many women are steeped in the fear of being alone, the fear of not being taken care of, the fear of not having another man on the hook in case the current one gets away. We can be so afraid of compromising tomorrow that we fail to take notice and celebrate the fact that we are standing firm today. 📖

4. Is it easier for you to imagine intimacy in a new relationship than to cultivate intimacy in the relationship you already have with your husband or with God? Why or why not?

5. Why do you think some women fear genuine intimacy (such as revealing our innermost thoughts to our husbands or to God), yet crave superficial intimacy (such as a rendezvous with an attractive stranger)?

6. How can we cultivate the courage to engage fully in genuine intimacy with our husbands and with God rather than seeking escape routes (fantasy, emotional affairs, and so on)?

🌿 GROWING TOGETHER
(Sharing the Truth in Small-Group Discussion)

> 📖 One day as I was beating myself up for yet another emotional affair, my best friend interrupted me with these sobering words: "Do you know what you are saying about the blood that Jesus shed for you when you refuse to forgive yourself for your past? You are saying that His blood wasn't good enough for you. It didn't have enough power to cleanse you." She was right. Underlying all of my self-pity was the belief that what Jesus did for me couldn't possibly be enough to rid me of my stain. I needed some special miracle to set me free, and until I got that miracle, I had to beat myself up as an act of penance. 📖

7. Why do you think it is much harder to forgive ourselves for mistakes in judgment than to forgive others?

8. What do you think God would say to the woman who can't seem to forgive herself? Do you know someone (including yourself) who needs to hear this message? How can you relay His feelings to her?

9. Of the three issues discussed in this chapter (past emotional pain, present pride, and future fear), which issue(s) did you recognize that you need to personally surrender? Why?

10. What victory is gained as a result of this surrender? How will you be affected by this victory? How does that make you feel and why?

∞

Lord, thank You for showing us that the way to victory is through surrendering our past emotional pain, our present prideful sins, and our future fear. Help us to let go of the things that hinder our spiritual growth and make us vulnerable to temptation. Free us to enjoy the sexual and emotional fulfillment that You desire for us to experience. In the name of Jesus. Amen.

rebuilding bridges

Read chapter 10 in *Every Woman's Battle*.

PLANTING GOOD SEEDS
(Personally Seeking God's Truth)

As you seek to cultivate a greater level of genuine intimacy in your marriage, some good seeds to plant in your heart include:

> For this reason a man will leave his father and mother and be
> united to his wife, and they will become one flesh. The man
> and his wife were both naked, and they felt no shame.
> (Genesis 2:24-25)

> My command is this: Love each other as I have loved you.
> Greater love has no one than this, that [she] lay down [her]
> life for [her] friends. (John 15:12-13)

1. Is your husband your closest, most intimate friend? If not, how specifically can you cultivate this kind of friendship? How would this benefit
you? your marriage?

As you consider any walls that separate you and your husband's feelings for
one another, a good seed to plant in your heart is James 5:16:

> Therefore confess your sins to each other and pray for each
> other so that you may be healed.

2. If confession is so good for an individual's soul, what effect can it have
on a couple? Why?

⚒ WEEDING OUT DECEPTION
(Recognizing the Truth)

> 📖 Imagine wanting to give a squirrel a nut. How would
> you do it? Would you chase the squirrel around the yard,
> grab him by his scrawny neck, and force the nut into his
> chubby cheeks? Of course not. You cannot require a squirrel
> to take a nut from you. However, you can inspire the squirrel
> to do this by simply placing a nut in your open palm, lying

down beneath a tree, and falling asleep. When it's the squirrel's idea to take the nut, he'll do it.

Communicating intimately with our husbands is very
similar to giving a squirrel a nut. Requiring it is futile. Intimacy can, however, be inspired. 📖

3. Have you attempted to force the issue of intimacy in your marriage?
   How, specifically, have you done this? Has it worked for you? Why or
   why not?

4. Through reading this chapter, what ideas have you gleaned for a more
   effective approach to cultivating intimacy?

📖 Discovering a new level of intimacy in your marriage may
be very difficult if you can't let your husband see completely
into you. As I mentioned previously, intimacy can best be
understood by breaking the word down into syllables: *in-to-
me-see*. Marital secrets serve no purpose but to alienate you
from the only one who can provide the level of intimacy you
truly desire as a sexual being. If you keep secrets from each
other, you may build a wall between you and ultimate sexual
and emotional fulfillment.

However, through humble confession and eventual
restoration of trust, you can turn those walls into bridges
that will bring the two of you closer together than ever
before. 📖

5. Have secrets formed a wall between you and ultimate fulfillment in
   your marriage relationship? If your husband could see into your mind
   and heart, would he find any surprises or bitter disappointments
   there? Why or why not?

6. If harboring a secret causes you to live in fear of your husband's knowing the truth, what effect does that have on you and your relationship?
   What do you fear most about being honest? Why?

7. If this fear became a reality, would it be any worse than living the rest
   of your life harboring secrets and undermining genuine intimacy in
   your marriage? Is the fulfillment you stand to gain worth the risk of
   being honest and letting him see into your heart and mind? Why or
   why not?

8. If your husband were to reveal all of the good, the bad, and the ugly
   in his heart and mind in an effort to cultivate genuine intimacy and
   accountability in your relationship, could you grant him the same
   grace that God grants to you? Is your love and commitment unconditional? Why or why not?

🐚 HARVESTING FULFILLMENT
(Applying the Truth)

📖 Genuine sexual intimacy involves all components of our
sexuality—the physical, mental, emotional, and spiritual.
When these four are combined, the result is an elixir that
stirs the soul, heals the heart, boggles the mind, and genu-
inely satisfies. 📖

📖 Once a woman experiences the intimacy of being mentally, emotionally, and spiritually naked before her husband
and feeling as if she is loved for who she truly is on the inside,
her natural response will be to want to give the outside package physically to her admirer. Notice I said *want to,* not *feel
that she has to.* Our desire to give our bodies as a trophy to
the man who has captivated our hearts and committed his
faithfulness to us sets the stage for genuine sexual fulfillment.
Sex performed merely out of obligation or duty will never
satisfy you (or him) like presenting your passion-filled mind,

body, heart, and soul to your husband on a silver platter, inviting your lover to come into your garden and taste its choice fruits (see Song of Songs 4:16). 📖

📖 God designed sex to be shared between two bodies, two minds, two hearts, and two spirits which unite together to become a one-flesh union. If you've never experienced this one-flesh union in your marriage, then you are missing out on one of the most earth-shattering and fulfilling moments of your life!

So how can you move from having "just sex" to experiencing a form of lovemaking that satisfies every fiber of your being? By understanding that sex is actually a form of worshiping God that a husband and wife enter into together. When two become one flesh physically, mentally, emotionally, and spiritually, they are saying to God, "Your plan for our sexual and emotional fulfillment is a good plan. We choose your plan instead of our own." 📖

9. Does reading these passages make you wonder if you have missed something in your sex life with your husband? If so, can you identify what specifically happens in the bedroom (either inside your mind or between the two of you) that hinders such sexual intimacy? How can that be overcome?

10. What would it take for you to *want* to give your mind, body, heart, and soul to your husband on a silver platter? Write your answer in the form of a prayer to God.

❧ GROWING TOGETHER
(Sharing the Truth in Small-Group Discussion)

Read through the "Intimacy Busters and Intimacy Boosters" chart at the close of chapter 10 on page 159. Then answer the following questions in a group or in smaller groups:

11. Which intimacy busters have you struggled with in the past?

12. How have you overcome those issues, and what advice do you have for other women currently struggling in those areas?

13. Which intimacy boosters have you discovered to be helpful? What effect have they had on your ultimate fulfillment? on your marriage relationship?

14. What intimacy busters could you add to this list? How do they affect couples? How can they be overcome?

15. What intimacy boosters might you add to this list? How can a woman implement those into her relationship? What benefits might result?

∞

*F*ather God, thank You for the incredible gift of sexual intimacy within marriage. We invite You to sanctify our bedrooms and help us enjoy being one flesh with our husbands. Help us to recognize walls that divide us and teach us how to turn those into bridges that reunite us. We ask this in Your Son's name. Amen.

retreating with the Lord

Read chapter 11 in *Every Woman's Battle*.

Planting Good Seeds
(Personally Seeking God's Truth)

As you cultivate a more intimate friendship with God, plant Proverbs 22:11 in your heart:

> [She] who loves a pure heart and whose speech is gracious
> will have the king for [her] friend.

1. On a scale of 1 to 10, how intimate do you feel your friendship with the Lord is? What would be required to increase that number?

As you consider the awesome privilege of being a child of the King, a good seed to plant in your heart is Galatians 4:4-6:

> God sent his Son, born of a woman, born under law, to redeem those under law, that we might receive the full rights of [daughters]. Because you are [daughters], God sent the Spirit of his Son into our hearts, the Spirit who calls out, "Abba, Father."

2. What does this verse mean to you? Why?

As you seek to embrace the magnitude of God's faithfulness, righteousness, and lavish love for you, some good seeds to plant in your heart are:

> I am my beloved's and my beloved is mine. (Song of Solomon 6:3, RSV)

> I will betroth you to me forever; I will betroth you in righteousness and justice, in love and compassion. I will betroth you in faithfulness, and you will acknowledge the LORD. (Hosea 2:19-20)

> Your love, O LORD, reaches to the heavens,
>   your faithfulness to the skies.
> Your righteousness is like the mighty mountains,
>   your justice like the great deep....
>   How priceless is your unfailing love!

Both high and low among [women]
>> find refuge in the shadow of your wings.
They feast on the abundance of your house;
>> you give them drink from your river of delights.
>> (Psalm 36:5-8)

3. Do you feel as if you are feasting on the abundance of God's house and drinking from His river of delights, or are you starving spiritually, wondering why you are unfulfilled in your relationships? Explain why you feel the way you do.

WEEDING OUT DECEPTION
(Recognizing the Truth)

The groom stood alone over in the corner of the room with his head down. As he stared at his ring, twisting the gold band that had just been placed on his finger by his bride, tears trickled down his cheeks and onto his hands. That is when I noticed the nail scars. The groom was Jesus.

He waited, but the bride never once turned her face toward her groom. She never held His hand. She never introduced the guests to Him. She operated independently of Him.

I awoke from my dream with a sick feeling in my stomach. "Lord, is this how I made you feel when I was looking

for love in all the wrong places?" I wept at the thought of
hurting Him so deeply.

Unfortunately, this dream illustrates exactly what is
happening between God and millions of His people. He
betroths Himself to us, we take His name (as "Christians"),
and then we go about our lives looking for love, attention,
and affection from every source under the sun except from
the Son of God, the Lover of our souls. 📖

4. In what ways do you identify with my dream above? Why?

5. Where do you look for love, attention, and affection? How successful
have you been in finding ultimate fulfillment from these sources?
What does God offer that other sources cannot?

🦃 HARVESTING FULFILLMENT
(Applying the Truth)

6. Of the following levels of intimacy with God discussed in this chapter, what is the most intimate level of relationship you've experienced with Him? What level are you currently experiencing and why?

Potter / Clay Relationship

Shepherd / Sheep Relationship

Master / Servant Relationship

Friend / Friend Relationship

Father / Daughter Relationship

Groom / Bride Relationship

7. If you are not currently at the level of relationship that you desire to be with God, what ideas from this chapter can you incorporate into your life in order to cultivate such intimacy? Are there others that you can add to this list?

____ a date night with Jesus

____ walking and talking with the Lord

____ a restful rendezvous with God

____ retreating with the Lord

____ other _____

____ other _____

8. If an actual retreat sounds inviting to you, circle the idea(s) that appeal to you most:

"Past, Present, and Future" Retreat—releasing past wounds through letters of forgiveness, examining present priorities, and evaluating future spiritual, relational, professional, financial, or physical goals.

Hobby Retreat—doing what you enjoy doing most (painting, reading, writing, and so on) while enjoying time alone with the Lord.

"Prayer, Praise, and Pampering" Retreat—giving yourself a spiritual spa treatment in preparation to enter His throne room in worship.

Intercessor's Retreat—praying for those God has laid on your heart and writing notes of encouragement.

"Thanks for the Memories" Retreat—updating your photo albums and giving thanks for all of the special friends and family who adorn the pages.

"Leaving a Legacy of Love" Retreat—reflecting on the spiritual markers of your life and communicating those in a special letter to your children.

9. Do you have other ideas for retreating with the Lord or specific ways you could honor Him with extended time? If so, what are they?

10. What are your biggest hindrances to pursuing extended time alone with God? How can those be overcome?

11. Specifically, what have you to gain from pursuing such experiences with Jesus? How will doing so bring victory in the battle for sexual and emotional fulfillment?

🌿 GROWING TOGETHER
(Sharing the Truth in Small-Group Discussion)

12. What in this chapter has been helpful to you, and how has it affected your thinking about intimacy with God?

📖 Response time is a vital part of my prayer life. He already knows what is on my heart without my saying a word. I need to make time to listen to what is on His heart because without listening I'll never have a clue. 📖

13. What percentage of your prayer time is spent talking to God, and what percentage is spent listening? If the same percentages were applied to an earthly friendship, what would the result be? Would there be mutual intimacy, or would the relationship feel one-sided?

14. Do you have a specific place, time of day, or activity that you engage in where you feel especially connected to God? If so, share that with the group.

15. If God spoke to you (or the entire group) right now, what do you think He would say? How would He say it? How would you respond?

📖 Anticipate [your retreat with the Lord] as an exciting date. You are running away with your Lover, not confining yourself to a convent. Be creative and bask in the beauty of intimate time alone with God.

However, let me warn you: *Experiencing this incredible pleasure can be very addictive.* My annual retreats have turned into far more frequent excursions. No human can meet our deepest needs like God can, nor should anyone be expected to. My husband doesn't mind granting me this time away because I come back revived, with a renewed sense of joy over being a bride of Christ and a fresh passion for being the wife and mother God has called me to be. I can think of no better way to spend my time. 📖

16. What are your deepest needs that no human can completely satisfy? Do you believe that God is capable of providing such satisfaction? If so, how can you allow Him to do so?

17. Use the space below to write a personal invitation to Jesus Christ, expressing your desire for Him to rendezvous with you on your next "date" or retreat. When will it be? Where? What would you like Him to do for you there?

18. What do you think Jesus' response will be? How does His response make you feel?

∞

Lord Jesus, we want our relationship with You to grow and blossom into everything You desire it to be. Help us to embrace our role as Your intimate friend, Your precious child, and Your chosen bride. Draw us into Your presence each day and fill us to overflowing with Your lavish love. In Your most holy name we pray. Amen.

all quiet on
the home front

Read chapter 12 in *Every Woman's Battle*.

ᴘʟᴀɴᴛɪɴɢ Gᴏᴏᴅ Sᴇᴇᴅs
(Personally Seeking God's Truth)

As you seek to cultivate the peace, hope and joy that comes from sexual and emotional integrity, a good seed to plant in your heart is Romans 15:13:

> May the God of hope fill you with all joy and peace as you
> trust in him, so that you may overflow with hope by the
> power of the Holy Spirit.

1. What do you need to trust God with so that you can experience joy and peace? How would trusting God with this part of your life give you hope?

As you pursue sexual fulfillment, plant Matthew 6:33 in your heart:

> Seek first his kingdom and his righteousness, and all these
> things will be given to you as well.

2. What does this verse mean to you? In what ways do you seek God first
in your life?

3. Does your time or your life need to be rearranged so that you are
seeking His kingdom and righteousness above all else? If so, how?

As you seek to overcome sexual and emotional compromise, a good seed to
plant in your heart is this:

> To [her] who overcomes, I will give the right to sit with me
> on my throne, just as I overcame and sat down with my
> Father on his throne. (Revelation 3:21)

4. Looking beyond this life and into eternity, describe what you believe
it will be like to sit as an overcomer with Jesus Christ on His throne.
How does imagining this picture inspire you to continue pursuing sex-

ual and emotional integrity? What can you do to ensure that you finish strong in this race toward righteousness?

WEEDING OUT DECEPTION
(Recognizing the Truth)

> 📖 I never realized how intense and chaotic my life was until
> I experienced the peace of living with sexual and emotional
> integrity. For years I had walked blindly into compromising
> situations, begged over dinner tables for morsels of affection,
> and found myself sleeping with the enemy time and time
> again. I consistently mistook intensity for intimacy and the
> concept of a peaceful relationship seemed unfathomable. 📖

5. As a result of reading this book, what things in your past do you recognize as being detrimental to your integrity and peace of mind? What effect were these issues having on you and your relationships?

6. How has your life become more peaceful as a result of avoiding such compromise? In what ways have you been strengthened as you pursue sexual integrity?

📖 I sat in a chair across from an imaginary "Shannon at fifteen" (the young girl I once was who was about to make all the sexual mistakes that I had just lived through). With my counselor's guidance, I was able to voice my new understanding of the pain and loneliness this fifteen-year-old had felt, sympathize with her naiveté and confusion about her sexual and emotional desires, and forgive her for the bad choices she was making and the pain that her poor judgment would cause me and many others. 📖

7. What do you know now that you wish you had known in your past relationships with men? What would you say to yourself if you could go back in time and speak face to face with that young woman?

🌾 HARVESTING FULFILLMENT
(Applying the Truth)

📖 I realize now that Craig was just as hurt over what I was thinking in my mind while we were having sex as I would have been if he had wanted to look at pornography while making love to me. Understanding how we each struggle to maintain sexual integrity has transformed our marriage, our bedroom in particular....

I did what you recommended.... We leave on a dim light and I open my eyes anytime I sense my mind wandering outside of our bedroom. It takes concentration, but when I relax and focus completely on Craig during sex and what we are experiencing together, I feel so close to him and so much closer to God as a result! I actually enjoy sex now rather than just tolerate it and let my mind wander. I never knew it could be this deeply gratifying. 📖

8. How has your deeper understanding of men and women's unique struggles with sexual integrity affected your relationship with your husband or the men you date?

9. Do you feel that you are (or will be) able to take off your mask and share your private sexual struggles with your marriage partner? Why or why not?

10. Does this level of openness and honesty with your husband make you feel any closer to God? If so, write your own prayer of thanksgiving. If not, write a prayer asking God to help you identify and remove any barriers that may still remain between you and Him.

🌾 GROWING TOGETHER
(Sharing the Truth in Small-Group Discussion)

11. What (or who) encouraged you to read *Every Woman's Battle* and go through this workbook? What were you hoping to find in its pages? What were your expectations, and were they fulfilled?

12. What did you discover in this study that you weren't expecting? How have these discoveries changed your life? your marriage? your relationships with the women in your discussion group?

📖 You will be tempted to resort to your old fantasies, your old masturbation habit, or your dysfunctional relational patterns. That doesn't mean that you can't have victory time and time again, however. With each thought taken captive, each inappropriate word not spoken, each extramarital advance you spurn, and each intimate sexual experience you enjoy with your husband, you will be reinforcing your victory and embracing God's plan for your sexual and emotional fulfillment. 📖

13. How will you know the difference between experiencing temptations and "crossing the line" in the future?

14. How can you ensure victory even though this battle will continue as long as your are living and breathing?

📖 To someone who knew the taste of defeat all too well,
the thrill of victory is truly something to be savored. 📖

15. Have you experienced the taste of defeat? Describe how it tastes.

16. Have you experienced the thrill of victory? Describe how it feels.

17. Do you know anyone with the taste of defeat on her tongue? If so, how can you share with her what victory tastes like and whet her appetite for God's plan for sexual and emotional integrity? Will you commit to pray for her and for God to use you to help bring victory into her life?

∞

Lord, thank You that Your plan for my sexual and emotional fulfillment is a perfect one. Continue revealing it to me and reminding me of it, especially when my determination to walk in integrity weakens. Strengthen me in times of temptation and give me a heart that recognizes and rejoices each time Your Holy Spirit guides me toward righteousness. Continue to cultivate genuine sexual intimacy between me and my husband and draw me into a deeper, more passionate love relationship with You day by day. Thank You for Your granting me peace, hope, and joy and teaching me how to be an overcomer. I look so forward to sitting next to You on Your throne for all eternity. In Jesus' most precious and holy name. Amen.

don't keep it to yourself

Congratulations on finishing this workbook! You are well on your way to winning the battle for sexual and emotional integrity. I pray that you have learned how to guard not just your body, but your mind, heart, and mouth from sexual compromise. I pray you have discovered God's plan for ultimate sexual fulfillment and that, if you are married, you are cultivating a deeper level of intimacy with your husband than you ever imagined possible. But most of all, I hope you have tasted and seen that, in fact, the Lord is good and His plans are perfect.

If you've just completed the *Every Woman's Battle Workbook* on your own and benefited from it, let me encourage you to consider inviting a group of other women together and leading them toward discovering God's plan for sexual and emotional fulfillment as well. This can help keep you accountable, but it will also enable you to encourage and help other women who are in the battle with you. If as women we can encourage each other to open up about our struggles in this area, we will be able to get the support and help we need.

You'll find more information about starting such a group on page 2 in the section titled "Questions You May Have About This Workbook."

about the author

Shannon Ethridge is a wife, mother, writer, speaker, lay counselor, and missionary for sexual wholeness. She has spoken to youth, college students, and adults since 1989, and her passions include instilling sexual values in children at an early age, challenging young people to embrace a life of sexual purity, ministering to women who have looked for love in the wrong places, and challenging all women to make Jesus Christ the primary Love of their life.

Shannon is also the founder of Women at the Well Ministries, which seeks to help women who are struggling with sex, love, and relationship issues, as well as to equip others to teach Women at the Well growth groups throughout the country and abroad.

A regular instructor on the Teen Mania Ministries Campus, Shannon has been featured numerous times on radio and television programs. She and her husband, Greg, have been married for thirteen years and live in a log cabin among the piney woods of east Texas with their two children, Erin (eleven) and Matthew (eight).

Women at the Well
Ministries

For speaking engagements or other resources available through Women at the Well Ministries, call 1-800-NEW-LIFE, go to www.everywomans battle.com, or e-mail Shannon at SEthridge@womanatthewell.com.

every man's battle workshops

from New Life Ministries

new Life Ministries receives hundreds of calls every month from Christian men who are struggling to stay pure in the midst of daily challenges to their sexual integrity and from pastors who are looking for guidance in how to keep fragile marriages from falling apart all around them.

As part of our commitment to equip individuals to win these battles, New Life Ministries has developed biblically based workshops directly geared to answer these needs. These workshops are held several times per year around the country.

- Our workshops **for men** are structured to equip men with the tools necessary to maintain sexual integrity and enjoy healthy, productive relationships.

- Our workshops **for church leaders** are targeted to help pastors and men's ministry leaders develop programs to help families being attacked by this destructive addiction.

Some comments from previous workshop attendees:

"An awesome, life-changing experience. Awesome teaching, teacher, content and program."　　　—DAVE

"God has truly worked a great work in me since the EMB workshop. I am fully confident that with God's help, I will be restored in my ministry position. Thank you for your concern. I realize that this is a battle, but I now have the weapons of warfare as mentioned in Ephesians 6:10, and I am using them to gain victory!"　　　—KEN

"It's great to have a workshop you can confidently recommend to anyone without hesitation, knowing that it is truly life changing. Your labors are not in vain!"　　　—DR. BRAD STENBERG, Pasadena, CA

If sexual temptation is threatening your marriage or your church, please call **1-800-NEW-LIFE** to speak with one of our specialists.